MIND-BENDING PUZZLES 2

by Terry Stickels

More Bushels of Brilliance to Boggle Your Brain!

Pomegranate
SAN FRANCISCO

FOREWORD BY **MICHAEL MICHALKO**

Published by Pomegranate Communications, Inc.
Box 6099, Rohnert Park, California 94927

Pomegranate Europe Ltd.
Fullbridge House, Fullbridge
Maldon, Essex CM9 4LE, England

Pomegranate Catalog No. A506
ISBN 0-7649-0691-7

Designed by Harrah Argentine

Printed in U.S.A.
07 06 05 04 03 02 01 00 99 98   10 9 8 7 6 5 4 3 2 1

First Edition

Terry Stickels's Mind-Bending Puzzles are also available in calendars and decks of Knowledge
Cards™, and in the book *Mind-Bending Puzzles Volume I,* all published by Pomegranate
Communications, Inc. For more information, please write to Pomegranate at Box 6099,
Rohnert Park, CA 94927; 800-227-1428 (www.pomegranate.com).

Foreword

I HAVE LONG BEEN one of Terry Stickels's most enthusiastic fans. I love to use his Mind-Bending Puzzles in my creativity seminars. Here's why: When most people are confronted with a problem, they usually refer to a similar situation in their past and try to apply the solution that worked back then. Essentially they ask themselves: What have I been taught—in life, education, or work—that will solve this problem? They then select the most promising approach based on their experience.

This kind of thinking short-circuits originality: If you always think the way you've always thought, you'll always get what you've always gotten: secondhand ideas. People who suffer from this rigidity of thought often fail when confronted by problems that are superficially similar to those they have encountered before, but which are really quite different.

In contrast, when creative thinkers are confronted with a problem, they approach it on its own terms. This willingness to consider a question in many ways is the quality that distinguishes the creative thinker. Terry Stickels's Mind-Bending Puzzles will help you expand your skills in creative thinking; you'll invent new ways of observing and thinking in order to solve these tricky brain-twisters. As they shock, surprise, and delight you, you'll find that you've joined me among Terry's many fans.

—Michael Michalko

Michael Michalko is author of *Thinkertoys (A Handbook of Business Creativity)*, *ThinkPak (A Brainstorming Card Set)*, and *Cracking Creativity (The Secrets of Creative Geniuses)*.

Welcome back!

Thank you for coming back for more Mind-Bending Puzzles in this second volume of all sorts of exercises for the brain. Just like Volume I, this book has a wide variety of puzzles to satisfy the diverse population of puzzle solvers. They can improve your thinking skills (in fact, my Mind-Bending Puzzles are used in a wide range of settings—from schools to corporate environments—to encourage creative problem solving) and provide hours of satisfying fun. I hope you enjoy solving these puzzles as much as I enjoyed making them up.

Please write to me in care of the publishers if you have any suggestions, criticisms, or questions about these puzzles. We love to hear from you, and we always want to keep adding to and improving on our puzzle publications. Your support of this publication and the Mind-Bending Puzzles calendars and decks of Knowledge Cards™ allows me to keep on my mind-bending path. Thank you.

Now, have fun!

—Terry Stickels

P.S. The answers appear on pages 85 to 92, followed by scribble pages for your creative work-outs. Also, if you happened to miss Volume I of *Mind-Bending Puzzles,* be sure to check it out!

Write to Terry c/o Pomegranate Communications, Inc., Box 6099, Rohnert Park, California 94927.

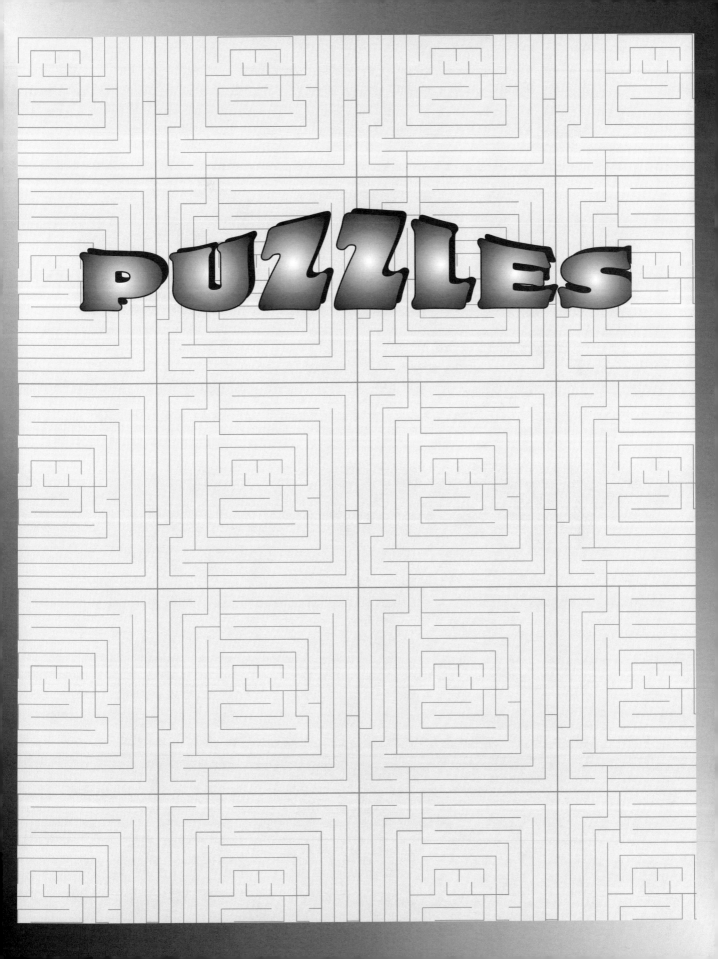

1.

If Molly's daughter is my daughter's mother, what am I to Molly?

> Grandmother
> Mother
> Daughter
> Granddaughter

 2.

Suppose all counting numbers were arranged in columns as shown below. Under what letter would the number 100 appear?

A	B	C	D	E	F	G
1	2	3	4	5	6	7
8	9	10	11	12	13	14
15	16	17	—	—	—	—

3.

Nancy and Audrey set out to cover a certain distance by foot. Nancy walks half the distance and runs half the distance, but Audrey walks half the time and runs half the time. Nancy and Audrey walk and run at the same rate. Who will reach the destination first (or will it be a tie)?

4.

Find the hidden phrase or title.

5.

The following seven numbers share a unique property. What is it?

1961   6889   6119   8008   8118   6699   6009

6.

In the puzzle below, the numbers in the second row are determined by the relationships of the numbers in the first row. Likewise, the numbers in the third row are determined by the relationships of the numbers in the second row. Can you determine the relationships and find the missing number?

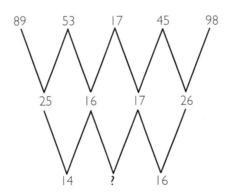

7.

A mathematician's will stated that his wife should get one-third of his estate, his son one-fifth, his older daughter one-sixth, and his younger daughter $9,000. Who received more, his older daughter or his younger daughter?

8.

What single-digit number should go in the box with the question mark?

6	5	9	2	7
1	4	3	5	?
8	0	2	8	1

 **9.**

In a store that sells clocks, I notice that most of them show different times. A grandfather clock reads 2:15, an alarm clock reads 2:35, a digital clock reads 2:00, and the store clock reads 2:23. The store clerk says that a clock in the corner has just been set correctly. It reads 2:17. What is the average number of minutes, fast or slow, that these five clocks are off?

 10.

Find the missing number in the following series:

$\frac{2}{3}$ $\frac{7}{12}$ $\frac{1}{2}$ $\frac{5}{12}$ $\frac{1}{3}$ $\frac{1}{4}$ $\frac{1}{6}$?

11.

Find the hidden phrase or title.

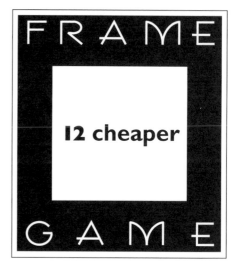

FRAME

12 cheaper

GAME

12.

While reading a newspaper you notice that four pages of one section are missing. One of the missing pages is page 5. The back page of this section is page 24. What are the other three missing pages?

 **13.**

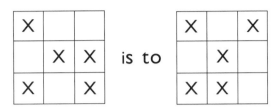

as

is to **?**

 **14.**

Below is a "trickle-down" word game. Change one letter and one letter only on each line to arrive at the word on the last line:

MOVE

_____

_____

_____

BARK

 **15.**

Suppose *a, b,* and *c* represent three positive whole numbers. If $a + b = 13$, $b + c = 22$, and $a + c = 19$, what is the value of *c*?

 16.

Sarah is older than Julie and Maggie. Maggie is older than Paula. Ann is younger than Julie but older than Paula. Ann is younger than Maggie. Sarah is younger than Liz. Who is the second oldest woman in this group?

17.

Find the hidden phrase or title.

FRAME

PRO MISE

GAME

 18.

What is the missing number in the following series?

13   7   18   10   5   ?   9   1   12   6

19.

How many triangles of any size are in the figure below?

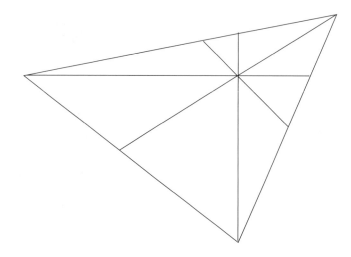

20.

Which of the following is the smallest?

a. $\dfrac{\sqrt{10}}{10}$

b. $\dfrac{1}{10}$

c. $\sqrt{10}$

d. $\dfrac{1}{\sqrt{10}}$

e. $\dfrac{1}{10\sqrt{10}}$

21.

Find the hidden phrase or title.

22.

Which is larger: 2^{73} or $2^{70} + 2^3$?

23.

There are four colored pencils—two blue, one green, and one yellow. If you drew two pencils from a drawer and you knew that one of them was blue, what would be the likelihood that the other pencil was also blue?

24.

Unscramble this word: KISDTYCRA

25.

Find the hidden phrase or title.

FRAME

_^juice

GAME

 26.

A certain blend of grass seed is made by mixing brand A ($8 a pound) with brand B ($5 a pound). If the blend is worth $6 a pound, how many pounds of brand A are needed to make 50 pounds of the blend?

27.

If you wrote down all the numbers from 1 to 100, how many times would you write the number 3?

 28.

Each of the following three words can have another three-letter word added to its beginning to form new words. Can you find at least one three-letter word to make this happen?

Ear

Less

Anger

29.

Find the hidden phrase or title.

30.

What is $3/4$ of $1/2$ of 4^2 minus $1/2$ of that result?

31.

Below are six discs stacked on a peg. The object is to reassemble the discs, one by one, in the same order on another peg, using the smallest number of moves. No larger disc can be placed on a smaller disc. How many moves will it take?

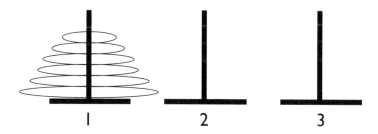

1   2   3

32.

Below is a list of numbers with accompanying codes. Can you decipher the code and determine the number on the last line?

Number	Code Number
589	521
724	386
1346	9764
?	485

33.

From the word "service," see if you can create 15 new words.

34.

Find the hidden phrase or title.

35.

Which is greater, a single discount of 12 percent or two successive discounts of 6 percent—or are they the same?

36.

Here's a fun and challenging puzzle for those who remember their algebra. Evaluate the following:

$$\frac{x + y}{x^2 + y^2} \cdot \frac{x}{x - y} \div \frac{(x + y)^2}{x^4 - y^4} - x$$

37.

The geometric figure below can be divided with one straight line into two parts that will fit together to make a perfect square. Draw that line by connecting two of the numbers.

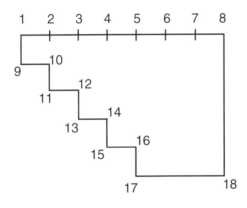

 38.

Find the hidden phrase or title.

39.

Some pibs are dals.
All dals are zons.
Some zons are rews.
Some rews are dals.
Therefore, some pibs are definitely rews.

Is the above conclusion true or false?

 40.

A cyclist can ride four different routes from East Klopper to Wickly. There are eight different routes from Wickly to Ganzoon. From Ganzoon to Poscatool, there are three different routes. How many different combinations of routes from East Klopper to Poscatool can the cyclist take? (Do not consider going directly from East Klopper to Poscatool: all routes pass through Wickly, Ganzoon, and Poscatool.)

 **41.**

Find the hidden phrase or title.

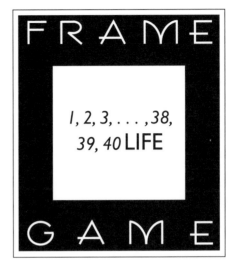

FRAME

1, 2, 3, . . . , 38,
39, 40 LIFE

GAME

 42.

The number six is considered a "perfect" number because its factors add up exactly to the number itself (3 + 2 + 1 = 6). What is the next perfect number?

27

43.

The *Genesee Flyer* leaves the station at 60 miles per hour. After 3 hours, the *Seneca Streamer* leaves the same station at 75 miles per hour, moving in the same direction on an adjacent track. Both trains depart the station at milepost 0. At what milepost will the *Streamer* draw even with the *Flyer*?

44.

Below is a sentence based on moving the letters of the alphabet in a consistent manner. See if you can crack the code and come up with the right answer.

BRX DUH D JHQLXV.

45.

The ratio of 3/7 to 4/9 is which of the following:

        a. 8/9
        b. 35/36
        c. 3/4
        d. 27/28
        I to I

 46.

Find the hidden phrase or title.

29

47.

Below is a teeter-totter with a 5-pound weight placed 10 feet from the fulcrum and a 6-pound weight placed 5 feet from the fulcrum. On the right side of the fulcrum is a 16-pound weight that needs to be placed in order to balance the weights on the left side. How many feet from the fulcrum should the 16-pound weight be placed?

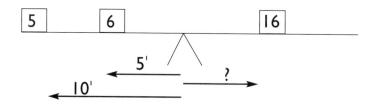

48.

Can you place a symbol between the two numbers below to create a number greater than 4 but less than 5?

4   5

49.

Kelsey has flipped a penny 17 times in a row, and every time it has landed on heads. What are the chances that the next throw will land on heads?

50.

The following puzzle is one of analytical reasoning. See if you can determine the relationships between the figures and the words to find solutions to the two unknowns.

$\triangle \triangle \triangle \triangle \triangle$ = PAG $\triangle \triangle \triangle \triangle$ = ?

$\square \square \square \square$ = PUF   MUFMAG = ?

$\begin{array}{c}\triangle \\ \triangle \\ \triangle \\ \triangle\end{array}$ = MAF

$\begin{array}{c}\square \\ \square \\ \square \\ \square \\ \square\end{array}$ = MUG

51.

Given the initial letters of the missing words, complete this sentence.

It is 212 D F at which W B.

52.

Find the hidden phrase or title.

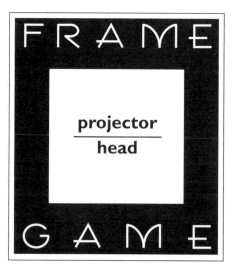

53.

Which is larger: one-third times one-third of a dozen dozen, or one-third dozen halved and cubed?

 54.

A box of chocolates can be divided equally among 3, 6, or 11 people. What is the smallest number of chocolates the box can contain?

55.

See if you can match each word in the left-hand column with its meaning in the right-hand column:

1. Unctuous	a. Study of the universe
2. Riparian	b. Relating to the bank of a lake or river
3. Porcine	c. An interlacing network, as of blood vessels
4. Plexus	d. An upright post
5. Platitude	e. Fertilize
6. Cosmology	f. Briskness
7. Concatenation	g. Relating to swine
8. Alacrity	h. A series connected by links
9. Fecundate	i. A trite remark
10. Newel	j. Oily

56.

Find the hidden phrase or title.

57.

Find the missing letter in the following series:

2   T   4   F   8   E   16   S   32   T   64   ?

 58.

Which figure does not belong with the other four figures?

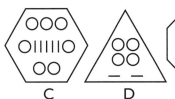

A   B   C   D   E

59.

I recently returned from a trip. Today is Friday. I returned four days before the day after the day before tomorrow. On what day did I return?

60.

Find the hidden phrase or title.

61.

A microscopic slide has 7,500 bacteria dying at a rate of 150 per hour. Another slide has 4,500 bacteria increasing at a rate of 50 per hour. In how many hours will the bacteria count on both slides be the same?

62.

A man told his friend, "Four years from now I'll be twice as old as I was fourteen years ago." How old is the man?

63.

Which figure does not belong with the others, and why?

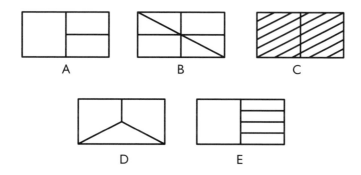

64.

Find the hidden phrase or title.

65.

Sometimes things that are mathematically or scientifically true seem impossible. You may think this is one of them. Can you guess what a cubic yard of water weighs?

17 pounds
170 pounds
1,700 pounds
500 pounds
98.8 pounds

66.

The probability of drawing the Ace of Spaces from a deck of 52 playing cards is 1 in 52. What is the probability of drawing the Ace, King, and Queen of spades on three consecutive draws?

67.

In this "trickle down" puzzle, you must change one letter of each succeeding word, starting at the top, to arrive at the word at the bottom. There may be more than one way to solve this—use your creativity!

PART

_____

_____

_____

WINE

 68.

Find the hidden phrase or title.

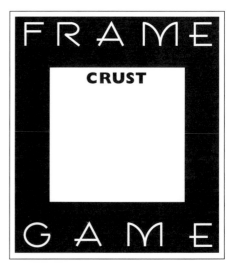

69.

Solve this puzzle without using a pencil or calculator:

$$1 \cdot 1 = 1$$
$$11 \cdot 11 = 121$$
$$111 \cdot 111 = 12{,}321$$
$$1{,}111 \cdot 1{,}111 = ?$$

70.

If 1/2 of 24 were 8, what would 1/3 of 18 be?

71.

If a team wins 60 percent of its games in the first third of a season, what percentage of the remaining games must it win to finish the season having won 80 percent of the games?

 72.

Find the hidden phrase or title.

73.

Given the initial letters of the missing words, complete the following sentence.

There are 50 S in the U S F.

74.

What is the missing number in the triangle on the right?

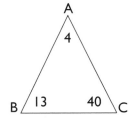 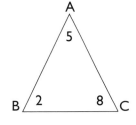 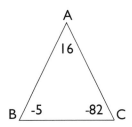 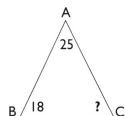

75.

There are six murks in a bop, eight bops in a farg, and three fargs in a yump. What is the number of murks in a yump divided by the number of bops in a yump?

76.

Find the hidden phrase or title.

77.

If the volume of a cube is 729 cubic feet, how many cubic yards is it?

78.

If three pears and four oranges cost $.39 and four pears and three oranges cost $.38, how much does one pear cost?

79.

What is the missing number in this grid?

15	81	168
23	111	?
5	27	56

 80.

Find the hidden phrase or title.

81.

A six-piece band has agreed that the entire band will be paid $1,225 per gig. But the leader of the band is paid twice as much as each of the other five musicians. How much does the leader earn each gig?

82.

In a foreign language, *fol birta klar* means "shine red apples." *Pirt klar farn* means "big red bicycles," and *obirts fol pirt* means "shine bicycles often." How would you say "big apples" in this language?

83.

What's the missing number next to the letter "E"?

P7   H4   O6   N6   E?

84.

If I quadrupled one-fifth of a fraction and multiplied it by that fraction, I would get one-fifth. What is the original fraction? (Hint: There are two answers.)

85.

Find the hidden phrase or title.

86.

Find three consecutive numbers such that the sum of the first number and the third number is 124.

87.

What nine-letter word is written in the square below? You may start at any letter and go in any direction, but don't go back over any letter.

$$
\begin{array}{ccc}
T & E & M \\
R & C & O \\
I & G & E
\end{array}
$$

 88.

At a reception, one-fourth of the guests departed at a certain time. Later, two-fifths of the remaining guests departed. Even later, three-fourths of those guests departed. If nine people were left, how many were originally at the party?

89.

Find the hidden phrase or title.

90.

Can you position four squares of equal size in such a way that you end up with five squares of equal size?

91.

If $16_a = 20$ and $36_a = 32$, what does 26_a equal?

92.

Find the hidden phrase or title.

93.

In spelling out numbers, you don't often find the letter "a." Quickly now, what is the first number, counting upward from zero, in which this letter appears?

 94.

With five fair tosses of a penny, what is the probability of its landing on heads five times in a row? (Hint: Remember, the tosses constitute a sequence of events.)

95.

What physical characteristic do the following capital letters share in common?

A H I M O T U V W X Y

96.

A triangle has sides of *X*, *Y*, and *Z*. Which of the following statements is true?

    1. $X - Y$ is always equal to 2.
    2. $Y - X$ is always less than Z.
    3. $Z - X$ is always greater than Y.
    4. $X + Y$ is always greater than $Z + Y$.
    5. No correct answer is given.

97.

What comes next in the following series?

240   120   40   10   2   ?

98.

Find the hidden phrase or title.

99.

What is the missing number in the circle below?

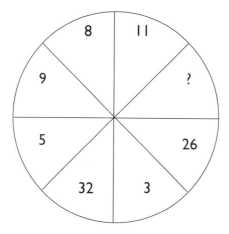

100.

Given four points in space and connecting three points at a time to determine a plane (extending to infinity), what is the maximum number of lines that will result from all intersections?

101.

When purchased together, a pair of binoculars and the case cost $100. If the binoculars cost $90 more than the case, how much does the case cost? Give yourself about 15 seconds to solve this.

102.

Find the hidden phrase or title.

103.

In this "trickle-down" puzzle, start at the top and change one letter to each succeeding word to arrive at the word at the bottom.

FAST

———

———

———

MIND

104.

A cube measuring four inches on each side is painted blue all over and is then sliced into one-inch cubes. How many of the smaller cubes are blue on three sides?

105.

Find the hidden phrase or title.

FRAME

R◆UGH

GAME

106.

A clock strikes six in five seconds. How long will it take to strike eleven?

107.

Sammy Johnson has two sisters, but the Johnson girls have no brother. How can this be?

 108.

Decipher this cryptogram:

T'M QPFASQ RS TD LATOPMSOLATP.
—G. N. KTSOMY

109.

Given the initial letters of the missing words, complete this sentence.

There are 9 I in a B G.

110.

Find the hidden phrase or title.

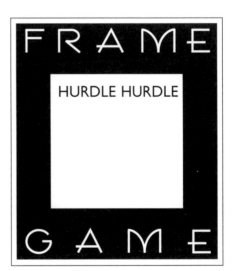

 **III.**

Imagine we were to adopt a new number system based on 13 instead of 10. Show a way in which the first 13 numbers might be written.

 **II2.**

What three-letter word can be placed in front of each of the following words to make four new words?

MAN
HOUSE
CAP
AM

 **113.**

How many squares of any size are in the figure below? Be careful; there may be more than you think!

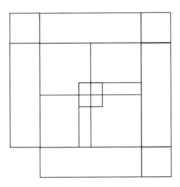

 **114.**

Electric current is measured in amps, resistance is measured in ohms, and power is measured in watts. What is frequency measured in?

115.

Find the hidden phrase or title.

FRAME

HOME

GAME

116.

Unscramble the following word:

LAMPANETRYARI

117.

What is the missing letter in the last circle?

118.

If 2,048 people entered a statewide singles tennis tournament, how many total matches would be played, including the championship match?

 **119.**

Find the hidden phrase or title.

FRAME

Omphe Omphe Omphe

GAME

 120.

A wine maker poured some wine into a large container. If three-fourths of the volume of wine in the container was equal to three-fifths of the empty space in the container, was the container less than half full or more than half full?

121.

Decipher this cryptogram phrase:

SEO LXABXGS JW EMLLGQOBB.

122.

Find the hidden phrase or title.

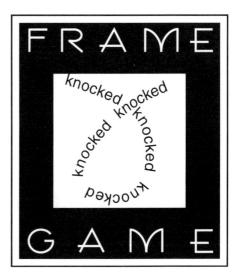

123.

The numbers in each box below have a relationship in common. Can you identify that relationship and find the missing number?

2, 11	4, 67	5, 128	3, ?

124.

How many triangles can you find in this diagram?

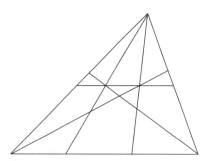

125.

What four-letter word can be placed in front of each of the following words to form new words?

LINE
PHONE
WATERS

126.

If you have a two-in-five chance of winning something, what are your odds?

127.

Find the hidden phrase or title.

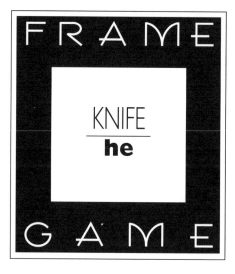

FRAME

KNIFE
___
he

GAME

128.

See if you can match the legal terms in the left column with the definitions in the right column:

1. Arbitration
2. Exculpatory
3. Judicial notice
4. Laches
5. Probative
6. Tort
7. Mediation

a. A rule in which the court takes notice of facts that are known with certainty to be true

b. Submission of controversies to a third party, whose decisions are usually binding

c. A doctrine providing a party an equitable defense where neglected rights are sought to be enforced against the party

d. A method of settling disputes with a neutral party in which the neutral party is a link between the disputing parties

e. A type of evidence that tends to clear or excuse a defendant from fault

f. Tending to prove a proposition or to persuade one of the truth of an allegation

g. A private or civil wrong

129.

The series below, containing the numbers 1 through 10, can be completed by placing the missing numbers, 2 and 3, at the end. Which comes first, the 2 or the 3? Why?

8   5   4   9   1   7   6   10   ?   ?

130.

Complete the following analogy:

B-sharp is to C as Bach is to ?

131.

Find the hidden phrase or title.

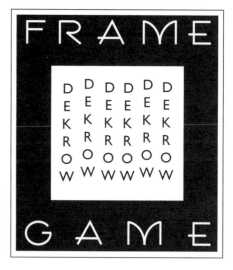

132.

How many different words can you make from the word "numbers"?

133.

Which figure below does not belong with the rest, and why?

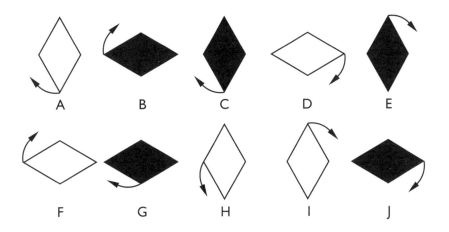

134.

Find the hidden phrase or title.

135.

Given the initial letters of the missing words, complete this sentence.

There are 6 P on the S of D.

136.

Find the hidden phrase or title.

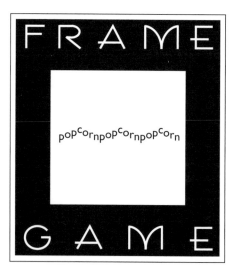

137.

Here's a four-letter "trickle-down" puzzle. See if you can come up with the three missing words, each with only one letter changed from the previous word, to arrive at the word KEEP. (There may be more than one set of correct answers.)

FEAR

‾‾‾‾

‾‾‾‾

‾‾‾‾

KEEP

 138.

What is the value of Z in the diagram below?

```
12        18        26        38        49
     X         8         X         X
         X         X         X
             X         X
                 Z
```

139.

How would you write 944 in Roman numerals?

 140.

Find the hidden phrase or title.

141.

Try your luck at this series. To arrive at each succeeding number, squaring of numbers is required.

0   6   6   20   20   42   42   ?

142.

Two of the five phrases listed below are equivalent. Which are they?

     a. 14 square yards
     b. 14 yards square
     c. 127 square feet
     d. 196 square yards
     e. 206 yards squared

143.

Given the initial letters of the missing words, complete this sentence.

There are 360 D in a S.

144.

Find the hidden phrase or title.

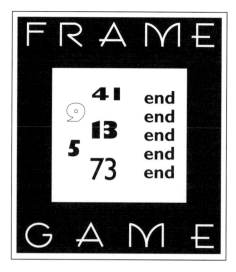

145.

A palindrome is a word or phrase spelled the same both forward and backward, such as noon, dad, deed, and sees. Can you think of three or more palindromic words of at least five letters?

146.

In a golf tournament, you're part of the final group on the last day. The first prize is $250,000. One member of the foursome (but not you!) sinks a 50-foot putt on the 72nd hole to win the tournament. You are ecstatic! In fact, that person is the one you hoped would win all along. You didn't have a bet on the outcome, so why are you happy that this golfer won?

147.

Find the hidden phrase or title.

148.

Unscramble the following word:

TESIALLEC

149.

If it were three hours later than it is now, it would be twice as long until midnight as it would be if it were four hours later. What time is it now?

150.

Change one letter of each succeeding word, starting at the top, to arrive at the word at the bottom.

MEAL

____

____

____

BOOK

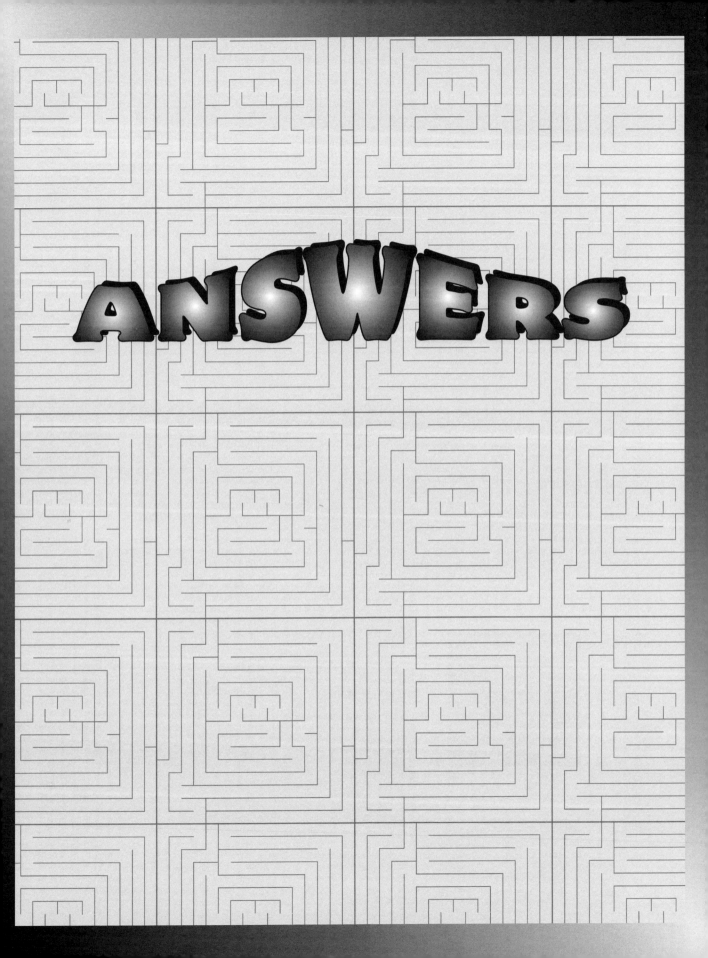

1. I am Molly's daughter.

2. It would appear in column B. Divide by 7 whatever number you wish to place and see what the remainder is. If the remainder is 1, the number goes in column A; if the remainder is 2, the number goes in column B; and so on. (If the remainder is zero, however, the number goes in column G.)

3. Audrey will reach the destination first. Suppose they cover 12 miles, both walking at a rate of 2 miles per hour and running at a rate of 6 miles per hour. Use the formula $rt = d$ (rate · time = distance) to find each person's time:

Nancy (walks half the distance and runs half the distance):

$$2t = 6 \text{ mi.}, \text{ so } t = 3 \text{ hrs. walking}$$
$$6t = 6 \text{ mi.}, \text{ so } t = 1 \text{ hr. running}$$
$$t = 4 \text{ hours total time}$$

Audrey (walks half the time and runs half the time):

$$2(\tfrac{1}{2}t) + 6(\tfrac{1}{2}t) = 12 \text{ mi.}$$
$$t + 3t = 12$$
$$4t = 12$$
$$t = 3 \text{ hours total time}$$

4. Lead by example.

5. Each reads the same when held upside down.

6. Simply add the sum of the two digits in any number to the sum of the two digits in the adjacent number to get the corresponding number in the row below. For example:

$$8 + 9 \ (89) \text{ and } 5 + 3 \ (53) = 25$$
$$5 + 3 \ (53) \text{ and } 1 + 7 \ (17) = 16$$

To find the missing number, add:

$$1 + 6 \ (16) \text{ and } 1 + 7 \ (17) = 15$$

7. His younger daughter received more—$4,000 more—than the older daughter. One way to solve this is to set up an equation that represents who received what:

$$x = \frac{1}{3}x + \frac{1}{5}x + \frac{1}{6}x + 9{,}000$$

$$x = \frac{10}{30}x + \frac{6}{30}x + \frac{5}{30}x + 9{,}000$$

$$x = \frac{21}{30}x + 9{,}000$$

Multiplying both sides of the equation by $^{30}\!/_{9}$, we get

$$\frac{30}{9}x = \frac{21}{9}x + \frac{270{,}000}{9}$$

$$\frac{30}{9}x - \frac{21}{9}x = 30{,}000$$

$$x = 30{,}000$$

Then

$$\frac{1}{3}x = \$10{,}000 \text{ (wife)}$$

$$\frac{1}{5}x = \$6{,}000 \text{ (son)}$$

$$\frac{1}{6}x = \$5{,}000 \text{ (older daughter)}$$

8. The missing number is 4. Simply add the first and second rows together to get the third row, like this:

```
  65,927
  14,354
  80,281
```

9. If you know that 2:17 is the correct time, find the difference, positive or negative, of the other clocks:

clock 1	2:15	− 2
clock 2	2:35	+18
clock 3	2:00	−17
clock 4	2:23	+ 6
clock 5	2:17	0
5 clocks		5 minutes

As a group, the clocks average 1 minute fast.

10. The answer is $^{1}\!/_{12}$. If you convert each fraction to 12ths, the series looks like this:

$$\frac{8}{12}, \ \frac{7}{12}, \ \frac{6}{12}, \ \frac{5}{12}, \ \frac{4}{12}, \ \frac{3}{12}, \ \frac{2}{12}, \ \frac{1}{12}$$

11. Cheaper by the dozen

12. Pages 6, 19, and 20 are also missing. Newspapers are printed double sided, two pages to a sheet. The first and second pages are attached to the second-to-last and last pages—in this case, pages 23 and 24. The rest of the pages are attached as follows:

1-2 with 23-24	7-8 with 17-18
3-4 with 21-22	9-10 with 15-16
5-6 with 19-20	11-12 with 13-14

13. Rotate the first square 90 degrees to the right to obtain the second square.

	X	
X		
		X

14.

```
MOVE
MORE
MARE
BARE
BARK
```

15. The value of c is 14. To solve the problem, set up the following equations:

$$(1)\ a + b = 13$$

$$(2)\ b + c = 22$$

$$(3)\ a + c = 19$$

Solve for b in equation (1):

$$b = 13 - a$$

Substitute this into equation (2):

$$13 - a + c = 22$$

$$-a + c = 9$$

Then combine equations (2) and (3) and solve for c:

$$-a + c = 9$$
$$a + c = 19$$
$$\overline{}$$
$$2c = 28$$
$$c = 14$$

16. Sarah is the second oldest; Liz is the oldest.

17. Broken promise

18. The missing number is 14. The first and last numbers added together make 19, as do the second number and the next-to-last number. Moving toward the middle in this fashion, each successive pair of numbers adds up to 19.

19. There are 23 triangles.

20. e.

$$\frac{1}{10\sqrt{10}}$$

21. You are out of touch.

22. 2^{73} is larger by a long way.

23. The chances are 1 in 5. The possibilities are:

$Blue_1$, $Blue_2$
$Blue_1$, Green
$Blue_1$, Yellow
$Blue_2$, Green
$Blue_2$, Yellow

24. Yardstick

25. Carrot juice (The symbol before "juice" is called a "caret.")

26. $17\frac{1}{3}$ lbs. Calculate the answer as follows:

$$1)\quad A + B = 50\ \text{lbs.}$$
$$\text{and}\quad 2)\quad \$8A + \$5B = 50 \cdot \$6$$

Then, multiply the first equation by −5, so:

$$-5A - 5B = -250$$

Next, combine with equation 2:

$$\$8A + \$5B = \$300$$
$$-5A - 5B = -250$$
$$\overline{}$$
$$3A = 50$$
$$A = 17\frac{1}{3}\ \text{lbs.}$$

27. The correct answer is 20. Don't forget that the number 33 has two 3s.

28. Place "end" at the beginning of each word:

> endear
> endless
> endanger

29. Your cup runneth over.

30. The answer is 3.

$$\frac{3}{4} \cdot \frac{1}{2} \cdot 16 = \frac{48}{8} = 6.$$

$$\frac{1}{2} \cdot 6 = 3; \quad 6 - 3 = 3.$$

31. It will take 63 moves. For any number of discs n, the number of moves can be found by $2^n - 1$.

32. The last number is 625. Subtract each individual digit in the numbers from 10 to crack the code.

33. Here's a list of 15 words. Are they anywhere near the words you came up with?

> serve
> vice
> rice
> ice
> see
> seer
> veer
> sieve
> eve
> rise
> ever
> sever
> cerise
> rive
> verse

34. Traffic congestion

35. A single discount of 12 percent is greater.

Here's an example:

$$12\% \cdot 100 = 12.00$$

then

$$6\% \cdot 100 = 6.00$$
$$100 - 6 = 94$$
$$6\% \cdot 94 = 5.64$$
$$6.00 + 5.64 = 11.64$$

12.00 is greater than 11.64

36. The answer is zero!

37. Draw a line from point 3 to point 12 and cut along the line to divide the figure. Turn the smaller figure upside-down, then connect points 1 and 12 on the smaller figure with points 17 and 13, respectively, on the larger figure.

38. An upward turn in the economy

39. False. Some pibs may be rews, but it is not definite.

40. The cyclist can take 96 ($4 \cdot 8 \cdot 3$) different routes.

41. Life begins at 40.

42. The next perfect number is 28 ($14 + 7 + 4 + 2 + 1 = 28$).

43. Milepost 900. To solve this problem, recall that rate · time = distance. Let x be the time it takes the *Seneca Streamer* to reach the milepost. Then:

$$60 \text{ mph} \cdot (x + 3) = 75 \text{ mph} \cdot x$$
$$60x + 180 = 75x$$
$$15x = 180$$
$$x = 12 \text{ hrs.}$$
$$75 \cdot 12 = 900 \text{ mi.}$$

44. YOU ARE A GENIUS. Move each of the letters in the puzzle back by three letters in the alphabet.

45. The correct answer is (d). To solve this, we need to find

$$\frac{^3/_7}{^4/_9}$$

Invert the denominator and multiply:

$$^3/_7 \cdot ^9/_4 = ^{27}/_{28}$$

46. Making up for lost time

47. The weight should be placed five feet from the fulcrum. First calculate foot-pounds on the left side:

$$(5 \cdot 10) + (6 \cdot 5) = 80 \text{ ft.-lbs.}$$

The right side must equal the left side:

$$16x = 80$$
$$x = 5$$

48. Place a decimal point between the two numbers to get 4.5.

49. Because there are two sides to the coin, the chances are always one in two.

50.

P = horizontal	△△△△ = PAF
A = triangle	MUFMAG = □
U = square	□
G = five	□
F = four	□
M = vertical	△
	△
	△
	△
	△

51. It is 212 degrees Fahrenheit at which water boils.

52. Overhead projector

53. The first calculation is $\frac{1}{3} \cdot \frac{1}{3}$ of $12 \cdot 12$, or $\frac{1}{9}$ of 144, which equals 16. The second calculation is $(12 \div 3 \div 2)^3$, or $(\frac{4}{2})^3$, or 2 cubed, which is 8. The correct answer is the first calculation.

54. There must be at least 66 chocolates—the least common denominator for 3, 6, and 11.

55.

1. Unctuous	j. Oily
2. Riparian	b. Relating to the bank of a lake or river
3. Porcine	g. Relating to swine
4. Plexus	c. An interlacing network
5. Platitude	i. A trite remark
6. Cosmology	a. Study of the universe
7. Concatenation	h. A series connected by links
8. Alacrity	f. Briskness
9. Fecundate	e. Fertilize
10. Newel	d. An upright post

56. I look up to you.

57. The missing letter is S. Each letter is the first letter of the preceding number when spelled out.

58. E. There is one more circle and one less straight line inside each figure than the number of sides to the figure—except for figure E. This eight-sided figure is the odd one out because it contains only six straight lines and only eight circles.

59. I returned on Tuesday. The day before tomorrow is today, Friday. The day after that is Saturday, and four days before Saturday is Tuesday.

60. Multiple personalities

61. 15 hours. The problem can be solved as follows:

$$7,500 - 150x = 4,500 + 50x$$
$$3,000 = 200x$$
$$x = 15$$

62. He is 32 years old. Here's the formula for the solution:

$$x + 4 = (x - 14) \cdot 2$$
$$x + 4 = 2x - 28$$
$$x = 32$$

63. D is the only figure that doesn't have a straight line dividing it in half.

64. Five-speed

65. It weighs approximately 1,700 pounds! One cubic foot of water weighs 62.4 pounds; one cubic yard (27 cubic feet) of water weighs 1,684.8 pounds.

66. The probability is 1 in 132,600.

$$\frac{1}{52} \cdot \frac{1}{51} \cdot \frac{1}{50} = \frac{1}{132,600}$$

67. Here's one way to solve the puzzle:

```
P A R T
WART
WANT
WANE
WINE
```

68. Upper crust

69. The answer is 1,234,321.

70. It would be 4. The best way to solve this is by setting up proportions:

$$\frac{\frac{1}{2} \cdot 24}{8} = \frac{\frac{1}{3} \cdot 18}{x}$$
$$\frac{12}{8} = \frac{6}{x}$$
$$12x = 48$$
$$x = 4$$

71. It must win 90 percent of the games. This is probably best expressed as follows: If a team wins 60 percent of one-third of the games, it is the same as winning 20 percent of all the games. Therefore,

$$20x + \frac{2}{3}x = 80x$$

$$\frac{2}{3}x = 60x$$

$$2x = 180$$

$$x = 90$$

72. Growing concern

73. There are 50 stars on the United States flag.

74. The missing number is 448. In each triangle, multiply A times B and subtract 2 to get C.

75. Six.

$$6m = b$$
$$8b = f$$
$$3f = y$$

We can find the number of bops in a yump by multiplying 8 · 3, or 24, and the number of murks in a yump by multiplying 24 times 6, or 144. So,

$$\frac{144 \text{ murks in a yump}}{24 \text{ bops in a yump}} = 6$$

76. Double play

77. It is 27 cubic yards—divide the number of cubic feet by 27 to get cubic yards.

78. A pear costs $.05. Here's one way to solve the problem. Letting p = pears and r = oranges, we have

(1) $\quad 3p + 4r = .39$

(2) $\quad 4p + 3r = .38$

Multiply equation (1) by 3 and equation (2) by –4:

$$9p + 12r = 1.17$$
$$\underline{-16p - 12r = -1.52}$$
$$-7p = -0.35$$

Now we can solve for p:

$$-7p = -.35$$
$$p = .05$$

79. 227. In each column, divide the top number by 3 to get the bottom number. Then add 3 to the sum of the top and bottom numbers to get the middle number.

80. Close encounters of the third kind

81. Think of it this way: If the leader receives twice as much as each of the others, that's the same as having seven members all earning the same amount, which would be $175 each. If the leader earns twice as much, he or she would therefore receive $350 per gig.

82. You would say *birta farn*. Notice that the adjectives follow the nouns.

klar	=	red
fol	=	shine
birta	=	apples
pirt	=	bicycles
farn	=	big
obirts	=	often

83. The missing number is 3. The numbers correspond to letters on the telephone keypad or dial.

84. $\frac{1}{2}$ or $-\frac{1}{2}$

$$\frac{1}{5}x \cdot 4 \cdot x = \frac{1}{5}$$

$$\frac{4x^2}{5} = \frac{1}{5}$$

$$4x^2 = 1$$

$$x^2 = \frac{1}{4}$$

$$x = \frac{1}{2} \text{ or} -\frac{1}{2}$$

85. Over and over again

86. The numbers are 61, 62, and 63. To solve this, let x be the first number; then $x + 1$ is the second number and $x + 2$ is the third number. An equation can be set up as follows:

$$x + (x + 2) = 124$$
$$2x + 2 = 124$$
$$2x = 122$$
$$x = 61$$

87. The word is "geometric."

88. 80 people. When ¼ of the guests left, ¾ of the people remained. When ⅖ of them left, ⅗ of ¾ remained. When ¾ of the remaining people left, ¼ of ⅗ of ¾ remained (⁹⁄₈₀). Since 9 people were left at the end:

$$\left(\frac{1}{4} \cdot \frac{3}{5} \cdot \frac{3}{4}\right)x = 9$$

$$\frac{9}{80}x = 9$$

$$x = 9 \cdot \frac{80}{9}$$

$$x = 80$$

89. Blood is thicker than water.

90.

	1	
2	5	3
	4	

91. It equals 26. The midpoint between 20 and 32 is 26, and the midpoint between 16_a and 36_a is 26.

$$16_a = 20$$

$$\text{Midpoint:} \quad 26_a = 26$$

$$36_a = 32$$

92. Stop in the name of love.

93. 1,000—one thousand!

94. The probability is $(\frac{1}{2})^5$, or 1 in 32.

95. If you hold any of these letters up to a mirror, it will appear exactly the same as on the page.

96. Statement (2) is true.

97. ⅓. In this series you take ½ of the previous number, then ⅓, ¼, ⅕, and finally ⅙. One-sixth of 2 equals ²⁄₆, or ⅓.

98. A bird in the hand is as good as two in the bush.

99. The missing number is 14. Pick any piece of the pie and look directly opposite that piece: the larger of the two numbers is 3 times the smaller number minus 1.

100. Six is the maximum number of lines.

101. The case costs $5; the binoculars cost $95. To solve this, let b = the binoculars and c = the case:

$$b + c = 100$$

$$b = 90 + c$$

Now substitute:

$$90 + c + c = 100$$

$$90 + 2c = 100$$

$$2c = 10$$

$$c = 5$$

102. Two eggs over easy

103.
FAST
FIST
MIST
MINT
MIND

104. Eight of the one-inch cubes have three blue sides—they were the corners of the four-inch cube.

105. A diamond in the rough

106. It will take ten seconds. Because the first strike sounds at zero seconds, two strikes sound in one second, three strikes in two, etc.

107. Sammy must be a girl.

108. I'd rather be in Philadelphia.

—W. C. Fields

109. There are nine innings in a baseball game.

110. High hurdles

111. It might look something like this:

1, 2, 3, 4, 5, 6, 7, 8, 9, ◇, ☆, ✱, 10

(Almost any symbols could be used to represent the old numbers 10, 11, and 12.) Our old number 13 now becomes 10. If you choose to call this number 10, the new symbols would need new names, as would all the numbers that contain these two symbols.

112. MAD

113. There are 17 squares.

114. Frequency is measured in hertz.

115. Home stretch

116. Parliamentary

117. The missing letter is R. Starting with the W in the first circle and moving counterclockwise in each successive circle, the words "What is the letter" are spelled out.

118. 2,047

119. Arc de Triomphe

120. The container was less than half full. If a is the amount of fluid in the container and b is the total volume of the container, $b - a$ = empty space. We can set up an equation as follows:

$$\frac{3}{4}a = \frac{3}{5}(b - a)$$

$$\frac{15}{4}a = 3b - 3a$$

$$15a = 12b - 12a$$

$$27a = 12b$$

$$9a = 4b$$

$$a = \frac{4}{9}b$$

121. The pursuit of happiness

122. Knocked for a loop

123. The second number in each box is the first number cubed plus three, so the missing number is 30.

124. There are 42 triangles.

125. Head

126. Your odds are 2 to 3:

Odds in favor of an event =

$$\frac{\text{Probability of favorable event}}{\text{Probability of unfavorable event}}$$

$$\frac{\frac{2}{5}}{\frac{3}{5}} = \frac{2}{3}$$

127. He went under the knife.

128. 1–b, 2–e, 3–a, 4–c, 5–f, 6–g, 7–d

129. 3, 2. The numbers are arranged in alphabetical order.

130. Bach. B-sharp and C are the same note.

131. All worked up

132. Here are 15. Can you come up with more?

burn
numb
bun
sum
run
nub
sun
um
runs
men
rum
muse
use
ruse
user

133. H is the only figure that is pointing counterclockwise.

134. Be on time.

135. There are six points on the Star of David.

136. Microwave popcorn

137.

    FEAR
    DEAR
    DEER
    DEEP
    KEEP

138. $Z = -7$

12		18		26		38		49
	6		8		12		11	
		2		4		-1		
			2		-5			
				-7				

The number in each row is found by subtracting the first of the two numbers above it from the second.

139. CMXLIV

140. William Tell Overture

141. The answer is 42. The series goes like this:

$1^2 - 1$, $2^2 + 2$, $3^2 - 3$, $4^2 + 4$, $5^2 - 5$, $6^2 + 6$, $7^2 - 7$, $8^2 + 8$, $9^2 - 9$, etc.

142. Phrases (b) and (d) are equivalent. "Fourteen yards square" describes a square measuring 14 yards by 14 yards, or 196 square yards.

143. There are 360 degrees in a square.

144. Odds and ends

145. madam
    level
    civic
    radar
    repaper
    deified
    rotator
    (and there are more)

146. You are the caddy, and your fee has probably just increased considerably.

147. Turn the other cheek.

148. Celestial

149. It is 7:00 P.M.

Let x = the time it is now, and y = the time until midnight:

$$x + 4 = 12 - y$$
$$\text{and}$$
$$x + 3 = 12 - 2y$$

Subtracting the second equation from the first, we get

$$1 = y$$
$$\text{Then,}$$
$$x + 4 = 11$$
$$x = 7$$

150. Here's one way:

    MEAL
    MEAT
    MOAT
    BOAT
    BOOT
    BOOK